W9-BEJ-824

Bannockburn School Dist. 106
2165 Telegraph Road
Bannockburn, Illinois 60015

HEALTHY HABITS

Rest and Sleep

Jayne Denshire

A+

Smart Apple Media
P.O. Box 3263
Mankato, MN, 56002

First published in 2010 by
MACMILLAN EDUCATION AUSTRALIA PTY LTD
15–19 Claremont St, South Yarra, Australia 3141

Visit our web site at www.macmillan.com.au or go directly to www.macmillanlibrary.com.au

Associated companies and representatives throughout the world.

Copyright © Jayne Denshire 2010

Library of Congress Cataloging-in-Publication Data

Denshire, Jayne.
Rest and sleep / Jayne Denshire.
    p. cm. — (Healthy habits)
Includes index.
ISBN 978-1-59920-550-2 (library binding)
1. Rest—Juvenile literature. 2. Sleep—Juvenile literature. I. Title.
RA786.D433 2011
613.7'9—dc22

                        2009038473

Edited by Helena Newton
Text and cover design by Kerri Wilson
Page layout by Domenic Lauricella
Photo research by Jes Senbergs
Illustrations by Richard Morden

Manufactured in China by Macmillan Production (Asia) Ltd.
Kwun Tong, Kowloon, Hong Kong
Supplier Code: CP December 2009

Acknowledgments
The author and the publisher are grateful to the following for permission to reproduce copyright material:

Front cover photograph: Boy sleeping, photo by © Leigh Schindler/iStockphoto

© Imagemore.co Ltd/Corbis, 17; © Jose Luis Pelaez/Corbis, 25 (bottom); © Olivia Baumgartner/Sygma/Corbis, 7 (middle); Absodels/Getty Images, 26; Dan Bigelow/Getty Images, 19; Julie Toy/Getty Images, 24; Yo/Getty Images, 11; iStockphoto, 6 (top); © Monika Adamczyk/iStockphoto, 18; © Janne Ahvo/iStockphoto, 13; © Blaney Photo/iStockphoto, 21; © Bogdan Pop/iStockphoto, 12; © Arkady Chubykin/iStockphoto, 3, 15; © Kim Gunkel/iStockphoto, 7 (bottom); © Sherwin McGehee/iStockphoto, 16; © Juan Monino/iStockphoto, 7 (top); © Glenda Powers/iStockphoto, 6 (bottom); © Leigh Schindler/iStockphoto, 1, 9; © Eva Serrabassa/iStockphoto, 20; Jupiter Images, 6 (middle), 8; Photolibrary © Imagebroker/Alamy, 5; Photolibrary © John Martin/Alamy, 23; Photolibrary © Gib Martinez/Alamy, 10; Photolibrary © RightImage/Alamy, 25 (top); Photolibrary © Stock Connection Distribution/Alamy, 22; © Monkey Business Images/Shutterstock, 4.

While every care has been taken to trace and acknowledge copyright, the publisher tenders their apologies for any accidental infringement where copyright has proved untraceable. Where the attempt has been unsuccessful, the publisher welcomes information that would redress the situation.

Contents

Healthy Habits 4

What Is Rest? 8

What Is Sleep? 9

Why Do You Need Rest? 10

Why Do You Need Sleep? 12

Stages of Sleep 14

Relaxation 18

Ways to Relax 20

Stress 22

People Who Help Us with Rest and Sleep 24

Make Rest and Sleep Healthy Habits 26

Try This Healthy Habit! 28

Amazing Sleep Facts 30

Glossary 31

Index 32

When a word is printed in **bold**, you can look up its meaning in the Glossary on page 31.

Healthy Habits

Healthy habits are actions we learn and understandings we develop. These actions and understandings help us be happy and healthy human beings.

Getting out in the fresh air is a healthy habit we can all learn.

If we do something often, we can carry out the action without thinking about it. This action is called a habit.

Putting on a hat every time you go out in the sun is a healthy habit.

Developing Healthy Habits

If we develop healthy habits when we are young, they become good choices for life. We can develop healthy habits in these six ways.

1 Exercise
Good exercise habits keep us fit and healthy.

2 Hygiene
Good **hygiene** habits keep us clean and healthy.

3 Nutrition
Good **nutrition** habits keep us growing and healthy.

4 Rest and sleep
Good rest and sleep habits keep us relaxed, energetic, and healthy.

5 Safety
Good safety habits keep us safe and healthy.

6 Well-being
Good **well-being** habits keep us feeling happy and healthy.

What Is Rest?

Rest is when you give your body time to relax.
You do not need to be asleep to rest.

Sitting quietly while reading a book is a good way to rest and relax.

What Is Sleep?

Sleep is a longer, deeper form of rest. When you are in a deep sleep, you are not aware of your thoughts. You do not respond to noises or movements.

When you sleep, you rest your senses as well as your body and mind.

Why Do You Need Rest?

You need to rest each day, because your brain and your body get tired. It is important for good health to rest your brain as well as your body.

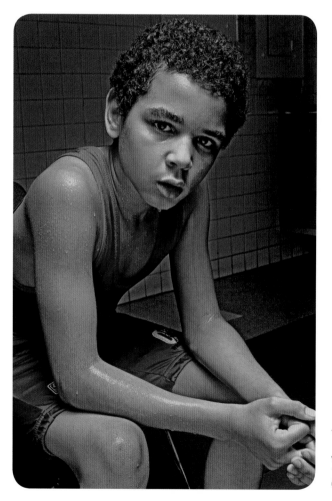

You need to rest your body after doing exercise.

Your body feels **physically** tired after moving around all day. Your brain feels **mentally** tired after a day of learning, talking, and thinking.

Working on your computer can make you mentally tired, so it is important to rest afterward.

Why Do You Need Sleep?

Sleep is the time when your mind and body are rebuilt and energized. While you are asleep, your body repairs itself and grows new **cells**.

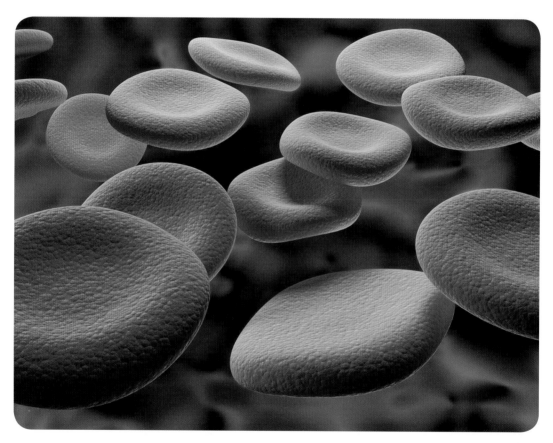

While you sleep, you grow new red blood cells (shown here close-up).

When you are asleep, your brain sorts through all your daily thoughts. Then it slows down for a while.

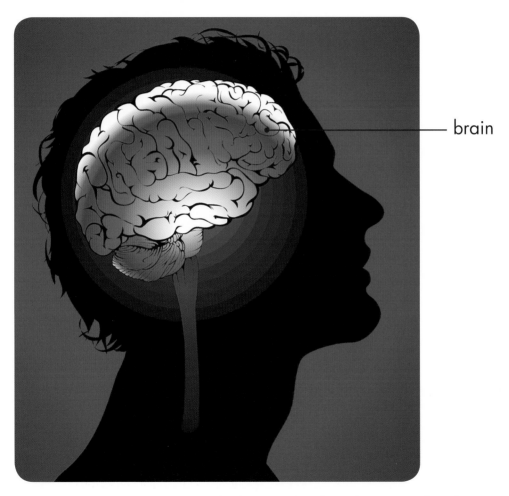

brain

While you sleep, your brain is repaired and reorganized.

Stages of Sleep

Your body goes through five different stages of sleep throughout the night. You move in and out of these stages several times a night.

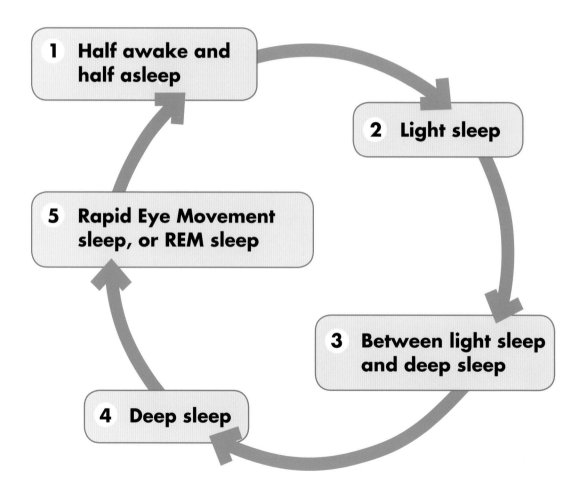

1 **Half awake and half asleep**

2 **Light sleep**

5 **Rapid Eye Movement sleep, or REM sleep**

3 **Between light sleep and deep sleep**

4 **Deep sleep**

Dreams

Dreams are images, thoughts, and feelings you have while you are sleeping. You mostly dream during the fifth stage of sleep, known as REM sleep.

During REM sleep, your eyes move rapidly under your eyelids, and your heart beats faster.

Catnaps

Catnaps are short sleeps during the day to refresh and relax you. They give you an energy boost.

Curling up for a catnap is a great way to energize your body and mind.

Power Naps

Power naps are short sleeps between activities when you are busy. They help you clear your mind and think more clearly again.

You do not always need to lie down to have a power nap.

Relaxation

Relaxation means taking a break and doing things that make you feel rested. When you are relaxed, you feel calm and less **stressed**.

Relaxation allows your body and mind to rest for a while.

When you relax, you usually slow down. Your body feels looser and your muscles do not feel tight.

It often helps you relax if you sit in a comfortable position on the floor.

Ways to Relax

There are many ways to relax. Some calm your body, some calm your mind, and some do both. Reading, listening to music, or doing a physical activity can relax you.

Swimming can help clear your mind after a busy day.

Many people learn special exercises and activities to relax. **Yoga**, **massage**, and **meditation** are some examples. They can help relax your mind and your body.

Doing yoga can help you move well and concentrate better.

Stress

Most people lead very busy lives. Often, the busier you are, the more stressed you feel. Stress puts extra strain on your body, which can be unhealthy.

Not being able to concentrate in class can be a sign of stress.

Ways to Lower Stress

It is important to lower your stress levels to stay healthy. You can do this by:

- taking regular breaks and vacations
- having some free time each day
- doing relaxing activities

You can lower your stress levels if you sit calmly and do something you enjoy.

People Who Help Us with Rest and Sleep

Some people have jobs working with rest and sleep. Meditation teachers, sleep **therapists**, and parents all try to help us rest and sleep.

Meditation teachers show people how to meditate. They teach people how to listen as they breathe in and out. This helps to relax the mind and body.

Sleep therapists help people who have problems sleeping. A sleep therapist determines how to help these people sleep better.

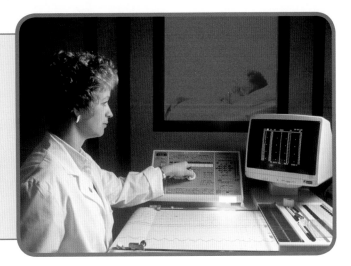

Parents often help their children with sleep. They read stories at bedtime and sing restful songs to help their children fall asleep.

Make Rest and Sleep Healthy Habits

Making rest and sleep healthy habits means finding time to relax and getting enough sleep. Good rest and sleep habits are important to stop you from feeling tired and unhealthy.

Doing relaxation exercises can help lower stress.

Healthy Rest and Sleep Checklist

This checklist shows how often you should do these healthy rest and sleep habits.

Healthy Rest and Sleep Habits	every day	whenever you can
have at least eight hours sleep	✔	
take a catnap		✔
rest your mind	✔	
take a break from the computer		✔
read a book quietly		✔
relax your mind and body	✔	
try some yoga or meditation		✔
massage your feet		✔
take a vacation		✔

Try This Healthy Habit!

Ask a partner to play "the relaxation game" with you. Read out loud this set of thoughts and movements. This will help your partner relax his or her mind and body.

You can ask a parent for help.

Read These Instructions to Your Partner:

1 Lie on your back.

2 Slowly roll your head from side to side.

3 Close your eyes.

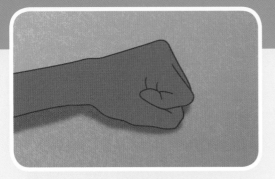

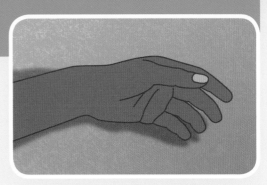

4 Think about each body part. Tighten your muscles, then relax them. Start at your toes and end at the top of your head.

5 Push all of the tightness out of your body.

6 Clear your mind of any thoughts.

After A Few Minutes, Say:

- Wriggle your fingers and toes and blink your eyes.
- Move your body around slowly, then sit up.
- Do you feel relaxed and refreshed?

Now swap positions with your partner. It is your turn to relax.

Amazing Sleep Facts

You spend one-third of each day in bed. So, you spend one-third of your life in bed!

A newborn baby needs twice as much sleep as a 10-year-old child.

Some people suffer from insomnia, which means they cannot get a healthy night's sleep.

You can change your sleeping position in bed up to 50 times a night.

Yawning makes more blood flow to the brain. After a yawn, you feel more **alert** again.

You spend 20 percent of your sleep time dreaming. On average, you spend about six years of your life dreaming!

Glossary

alert	wide awake
cells	the smallest living parts of a living thing
hygiene	what we do to keep ourselves clean and healthy
massage	rubbing or pressing on the body to relax it or ease pain
meditation	"letting go" of thoughts and feelings for relaxation
mentally	in the mind
nutrition	what our bodies take in and use from the food we eat
physically	in the body
stressed	feeling tense and unrelaxed
therapists	people who treat illnesses of the body or mind
well-being	a state of feeling healthy and happy
yoga	a system of exercises, breathing, and meditation

Index

b

brain   10, 11, 13, 30

c

calm   18, 20, 23

catnaps   16, 27

cells   12

d

dreams   15, 30

e

energy   7, 12, 16

exercise   6, 10, 21

m

massage   21, 27

meditation   21, 24, 27

meditation teachers   24

muscles   19, 29

n

naps   16–17, 27

nutrition   6

p

parents   24, 25

power naps   17

r

Rapid Eye Movement
   (REM) sleep   14, 15

reading   8, 20, 25, 27

relaxation   7, 8, 16, 18–21,
   23, 24, 26, 27, 28–29

relaxation exercises   26,
   28–29

rest   7, 8, 9, 10–11, 18, 24,
   26, 27

s

sleep   7, 9, 12–17, 24, 25,
   26, 27, 30

sleep therapists   24, 25

stages of sleep   14–15

stress   18, 22–23, 26

y

yoga   21, 27